For

March 2024

(Beryl Young was (Family) my neighbour in Victoria)

A BOY NAMED TOMMY DOUGLAS

STORY BY BERYL YOUNG
ILLUSTRATED BY JOAN STEACY

TOMMY RAN ACROSS THE FIELD AND BURST THROUGH THE BACK DOOR.

"MUM! MUM! I BASHED MY KNEE," HE CRIED.
BLOOD RAN DOWN TOMMY'S LEG. TEARS RAN DOWN HIS CHEEKS.
"IT REALLY HURTS," TOMMY GROANED.

"I TRIPPED AND HIT A SHARP STONE."

TOMMY SOBBED AS HIS MOTHER CLEANED THE WOUND. TOMMY WAS SMALL FOR HIS SEVEN YEARS, BUT HE LOVED RUNNING . . . FAST. HE'D HAD LOTS OF SCRAPES BEFORE, BUT THIS GASH WAS DEEP - RIGHT DOWN TO THE BONE.

TOMMY'S MOTHER BANDAGED THE WOUND. SHE HUGGED TOMMY AND BROUGHT HIM SOME MILK AND WARM OATCAKES.

THAT NIGHT, TOMMY'S FATHER SAID, "WE DON'T HAVE MONEY TO PAY A DOCTOR, SON. YOUR LEG WILL HEAL SOON."
"HE'S OUR BRAVE LAD," HIS MOTHER SAID.

TOMMY DIDN'T KNOW IT, BUT HE WAS GOING TO HAVE TO BE BRAVE FOR A VERY LONG TIME.

THE NEXT WINTER TOMMY STILL COULDN'T WALK. TWO OF HIS CLASSMATES CAME TO THE DOOR.

"WE'LL PULL TOMMY TO SCHOOL ON OUR SLEIGH," THEY SAID.

AT RECESS TOMMY STOOD AT THE CLASSROOM WINDOW AND WATCHED HIS FRIENDS PLAY HOCKEY AND BUILD SNOW FORTS.

IT WASN'T FAIR.

TOMMY DECIDED TO PRACTISE RECITING POEMS BY THE SCOTTISH POET ROBBIE BURNS. HIS FRIENDS CLAPPED AND CHEERED WHEN TOMMY PERFORMED AT SCHOOL CONCERTS.

THIS WAS SOMETHING HE COULD DO!

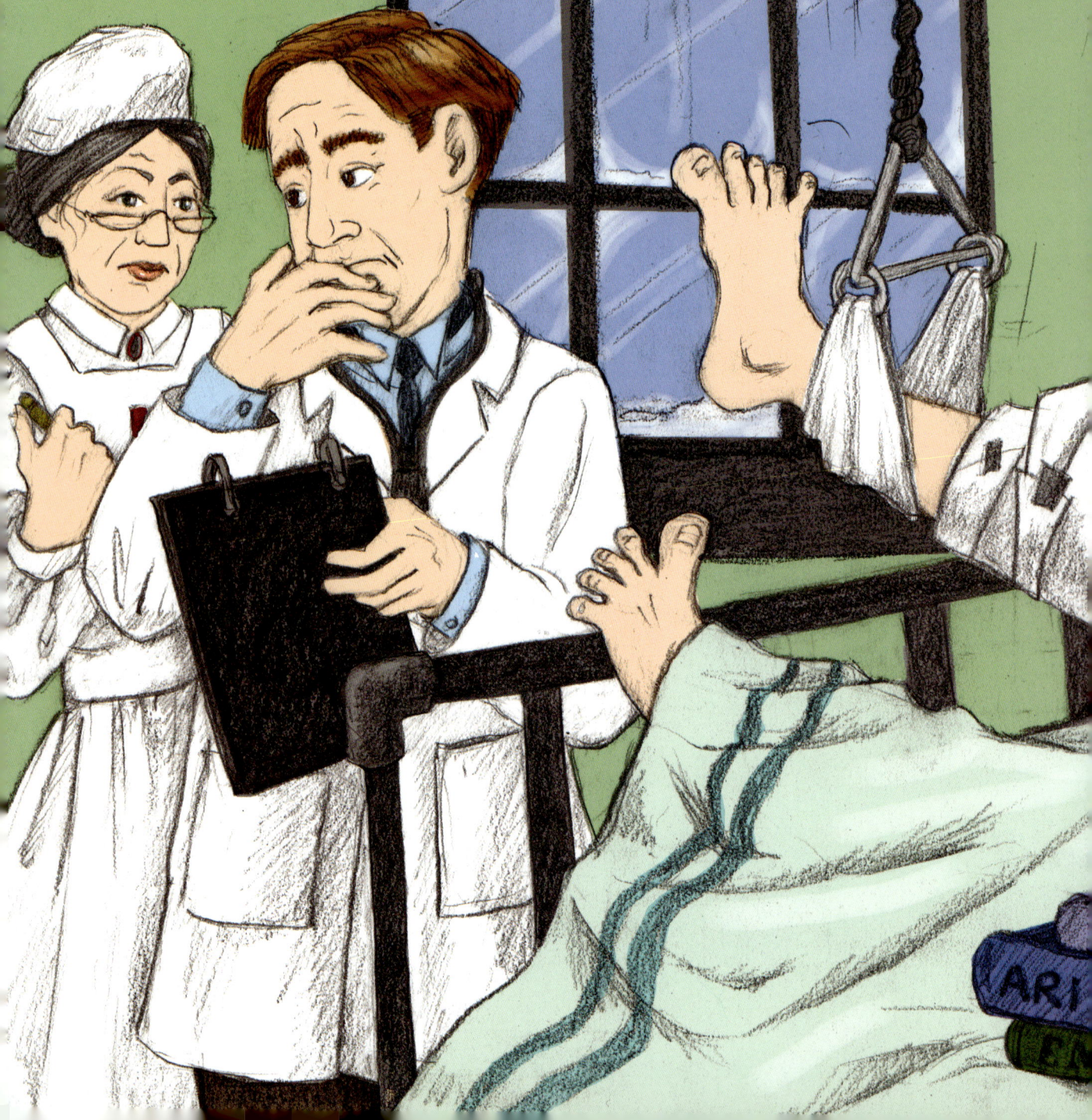

MONTHS WENT BY, BUT TOMMY'S LEG GOT WORSE.

"MY WHOLE LEG IS BURNING. FEELS LIKE IT'S ON FIRE," TOMMY TOLD HIS PARENTS. THEY DECIDED TO GET OUT THEIR SMALL SAVINGS TO TAKE TOMMY TO A DOCTOR.

"THERE'S AN INFECTION IN THE BOY'S BONE," THE DOCTOR SAID. "HE NEEDS COMPLETE HOSPITAL REST."

TOMMY STAYED IN THE HOSPITAL FOR WEEKS AND WEEKS. NONE OF HIS FRIENDS WERE ALLOWED TO VISIT. HE WAS LONELY AND MISERABLE.

THE DAYS AND NIGHTS DRAGGED ON. ONE DAY THE DOCTOR LOOKED SERIOUS.

"WE CAN'T WAIT ANY LONGER," HE SAID. "WE HAVE TO AMPUTATE TOMMY'S LEG."

AMPUTATE! TOMMY COULDN'T GET HIS BREATH. "YOU MEAN CUT MY LEG OFF?"
THE DOCTOR NODDED. "THE SURGERY WILL BE IN TWO DAYS."

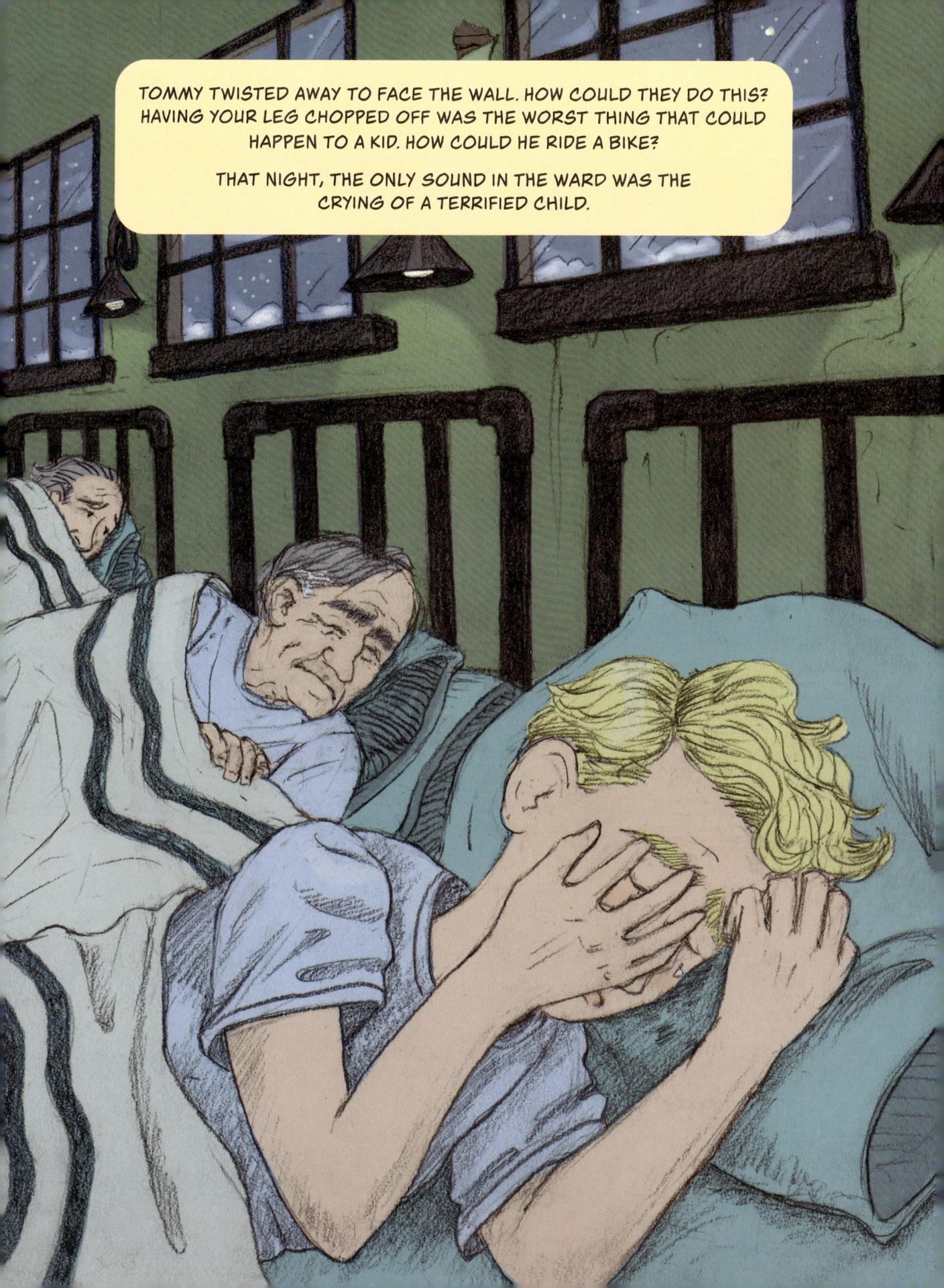

TOMMY TWISTED AWAY TO FACE THE WALL. HOW COULD THEY DO THIS? HAVING YOUR LEG CHOPPED OFF WAS THE WORST THING THAT COULD HAPPEN TO A KID. HOW COULD HE RIDE A BIKE?

THAT NIGHT, THE ONLY SOUND IN THE WARD WAS THE CRYING OF A TERRIFIED CHILD.

EARLY THE NEXT MORNING. DR. R.H. SMITH, A FAMOUS BONE SURGEON, WALKED INTO THE ROOM. A GROUP OF MEDICAL STUDENTS FOLLOWED HIM.

"WHY ARE YOU CRYING, YOUNG MAN?" DR. SMITH ASKED TOMMY. TOMMY COULD BARELY GET THE WORDS OUT. "THEY'RE GOING TO CUT MY LEG OFF."

DR. SMITH EXAMINED TOMMY'S KNEE. HE READ THE HOSPITAL CHART. "WELL, TOMMY," HE SAID, "I MIGHT BE ABLE TO SAVE YOUR LEG WITH AN OPERATION."

TOMMY'S HEART LEAPT, BUT HIS PARENTS SHOOK THEIR HEADS.
"WE HAVE NO MONEY TO PAY A SPECIALIST LIKE YOU."

DR. SMITH THOUGHT FOR A MINUTE. "TELL YOU WHAT," HE SAID. "I'LL DO THE SURGERY
AT NO COST IF YOU LET ME USE TOMMY'S CASE TO TEACH MY STUDENTS."

TOMMY COULDN'T BELIEVE IT.
"YES!" HE SHOUTED.

HIS PARENTS NODDED AT DR. SMITH.
TOMMY COULDN'T SLEEP THAT NIGHT.
THE SURGEON SAID HE MIGHT BE ABLE
TO SAVE THE LEG. HE DIDN'T PROMISE.

TOMMY FELT SLEEPY WHEN HE WOKE UP AFTER THE OPERATION. WAS HIS LEG STILL THERE? HE REACHED DOWN. YES, THERE IT WAS! BUT HAD THE DOCTOR FIXED HIS KNEE?

DR. SMITH CAME IN TWO DAYS LATER. TOMMY WATCHED HIS FACE CLOSELY. DR. SMITH BROKE INTO A BIG SMILE. "I'VE SAVED YOUR LEG, TOMMY," HE SAID, "BUT I'M SORRY YOU'LL NEVER BE ABLE TO BEND IT."

TOMMY GRINNED UP AT HIM.
"BUT I CAN, SIR. LOOK!"
"I'M GOING TO LEARN TO SKATE.
I WANT TO PLAY HOCKEY!"
TOMMY CHEERED, AS HE
THANKED DR. SMITH.

TOMMY NEVER FORGOT DR. SMITH.
OTHER CHILDREN WHO NEEDED MEDICAL
HELP WOULDN'T BE AS LUCKY AS HE'D
BEEN. HE THOUGHT ABOUT THAT A LOT.

IT WASN'T FAIR.

HOCKEY IMMORTALS

TOMMY DID LEARN TO SKATE AND HE DID PLAY HOCKEY.
HE LOVED TO FEEL THE COLD WIND ON HIS CHEEKS AS HE RACED
DOWN THE RINK. IT WAS GOOD TO BE STRONG AND HEALTHY.
AFTER HE GRADUATED FROM HIGH SCHOOL, TOMMY STUDIED
TO BE A PREACHER IN THE BAPTIST CHURCH.

THE DAY CAME WHEN TOMMY STOOD IN FRONT OF HIS FIRST CHURCH CONGREGATION IN WEYBURN, SASKATCHEWAN. "THIS CHURCH WON'T BE JUST FOR WORSHIP," HE SAID. "WE WILL HELP PEOPLE IN OUR COMMUNITY."

A YOUNG WOMAN CALLED IRMA CAME TO THE CHURCH. SHE LIKED THE YOUNG MINISTER'S SMILE AND SHE LIKED WHAT HE SAID. IN A SHORT TIME THEY WERE MARRIED.

IT WAS THE 1930s AND THINGS WERE CHANGING IN CANADA.
EVERY DAY PEOPLE WERE DESPERATE. THEY DIDN'T HAVE JOBS.
THEY DIDN'T HAVE ENOUGH FOOD TO FEED THEIR FAMILIES.
THEY CERTAINLY COULD NOT PAY FOR A DOCTOR'S CARE IF THEY FELL SICK.

ONE DAY, A FARMER TOLD TOMMY THAT HIS FOURTEEN-YEAR-OLD
DAUGHTER HAD DIED OF A BURST APPENDIX. THE MAN WAS WEEPING.
"WE DIDN'T HAVE THE MONEY TO PAY A DOCTOR. THEN IT WAS TOO LATE."

TOMMY KNEW THAT WASN'T RIGHT.

IT MADE HIM THINK. MAYBE HE COULD DO MORE TO HELP PEOPLE AS A POLITICIAN THAN AS A CHURCH MINISTER. "I SHOULD BE IN GOVERNMENT," HE TOLD IRMA. "I COULD WORK TO PASS LAWS TO HELP PEOPLE."

BUT FIRST, TOMMY HAD TO CAMPAIGN TO CONVINCE PEOPLE TO VOTE FOR HIM. HE TRAVELLED ALL OVER THE PROVINCE, SPEAKING IN TOWN HALLS, AT PICNICS AND RALLIES.

TOMMY WAS A WONDERFUL SPEAKER. HIS YEARS RECITING POEMS AS A BOY HAD TAUGHT HIM HOW TO INSPIRE A CROWD! PEOPLE LIKED TOMMY. THEY BELIEVED IN HIS DREAM OF MEDICAL CARE FOR EVERYONE.

TOMMY WON THE ELECTION WITH A BIG VICTORY AND BECAME PREMIER OF SASKATCHEWAN.

HE BEGAN TO WORK TO CHANGE THE LAW ABOUT HEALTH CARE. IT TOOK A LONG TIME. FIFTEEN YEARS! THE DAY CAME WHEN THE GOVERNMENT VOTED. ON JULY 1, 1962, THE VOTE PASSED! TOMMY PROUDLY CALLED HIS NEW PLAN MEDICARE.

NOW EVERYONE IN THE PROVINCE WOULD HAVE MEDICAL CARE FROM A DOCTOR. EVEN FROM A SPECIALIST LIKE DR. SMITH, THE SURGEON WHO HAD SAVED TOMMY'S LEG.

TOMMY'S DREAM HAD COME TRUE FOR THE PEOPLE OF SASKATCHEWAN.

NOW TOMMY HAD AN EVEN BIGGER DREAM.

HE BECAME THE LEADER OF THE NEW DEMOCRATIC PARTY IN OTTAWA. AFTER SIX MORE YEARS OF PLANNING AND DEBATING, FINALLY IN 1968, MEDICARE WAS AVAILABLE TO ALL CANADIANS. TODAY, IF A CHILD IN HALIFAX IS DIAGNOSED WITH CANCER AND NEEDS MONTHS OF EXPENSIVE TREATMENTS, HIS PARENTS DON'T HAVE TO WORRY ABOUT PAYING. IT'S ALL FREE.

TODAY, IF A BABY IN IQALUIT IS BORN WITH A WEAK HEART, AN AIR AMBULANCE PLANE WILL FLY THE BABY TO TORONTO FOR HEART SURGERY.

TODAY EVERY CANADIAN, YOUNG OR OLD, RICH OR POOR, WHETHER THEY LIVE IN A TOWN OR IN THE COUNTRY, IN THE SOUTH OR IN THE NORTH, HAS THE MEDICAL CARE THEY NEED.

THE BOY NAMED TOMMY DOUGLAS BECAME
THE MAN WHO CHANGED THE WORLD FOR CANADIANS.
THEY CALL HIM THE FATHER OF MEDICARE.

ABOUT TOMMY DOUGLAS

*"MY DREAM IS FOR PEOPLE AROUND THE WORLD TO LOOK UP AND SEE
CANADA LIKE A LITTLE JEWEL SITTING AT THE TOP OF THE CONTINENT"*
TOMMY DOUGLAS TO HIS TEENAGE DAUGHTER SHIRLEY

THOMAS CLEMENT DOUGLAS WAS BORN ON OCTOBER 20, 1904, IN FALKIRK, SCOTLAND. WHEN HE WAS SEVEN, TOMMY'S FAMILY MOVED TO CANADA TO LIVE IN WINNIPEG, MANITOBA. HIS FATHER HAD A JOB AS AN IRON WORKER, BUT THE FAMILY DID NOT HAVE A LOT OF MONEY. THE FIRST CHRISTMAS TOMMY AND HIS TWO SISTERS HAD TO SHARE ONE PRESENT – A BOARD GAME OF CHECKERS.

THAT YEAR TOMMY INJURED HIS RIGHT KNEE WHICH DEVELOPED INTO A SERIOUS INFECTION CALLED OSTEOMYELITIS. TOMMY WAS TEN YEARS OLD WHEN DR. R. H. SMITH OPERATED THREE TIMES ON HIS LEG AND SAVED IT FROM AMPUTATION.

TOMMY LEFT SCHOOL AT FOURTEEN TO EARN MONEY TO HELP HIS FAMILY BY WORKING AS AN APPRENTICE PRINTER. HE ALSO TRAINED AS A BOXER AND SURPRISINGLY WON THE LIGHTWEIGHT BOXING CHAMPIONSHIP OF MANITOBA TWO YEARS IN A ROW.

TOMMY DECIDED TO RETURN TO HIGH SCHOOL AND THEN ATTENDED BRANDON THEOLOGICAL COLLEGE. HE BECAME THE MINISTER AT CALVARY BAPTIST CHURCH IN WEYBURN, SASKATCHEWAN. HE AND HIS WIFE IRMA HAD TWO DAUGHTERS, SHIRLEY AND JOAN.

IN 1932, THE CO-OPERATIVE COMMONWEALTH FEDERATION (CCF) WAS FORMED AS A POLITICAL PARTY. TOMMY SHARED THEIR SOCIAL DEMOCRATIC BELIEFS THAT GOVERNMENTS SHOULD CREATE JOBS, CARE FOR OLDER PEOPLE, AND PROVIDE MEDICAL CARE FOR EVERYONE WHO NEEDED IT. TOMMY CAMPAIGNED TO BECOME A MEMBER OF PARLIAMENT. PEOPLE LOVED THE IDEAS IN HIS FIERY SPEECHES, AND THEY CALLED HIM TOMMY, NEVER TOM. EVERY WEEK HE HAD A RADIO BROADCAST AND ENDED WITH "MY FRIENDS, WATCH OUT FOR THE LITTLE FELLOW WITH AN IDEA."

TOMMY WON THE ELECTION AND BECAME A CCF MEMBER OF PARLIAMENT IN OTTAWA, AND LATER, PREMIER OF SASKATCHEWAN. IT WAS 1944 AND THIS WAS THE FIRST SOCIAL DEMOCRATIC GOVERNMENT ELECTED IN NORTH AMERICA.

SLOWLY OVER SEVENTEEN YEARS, TOMMY'S GOVERNMENT PLANNED FOR MEDICAL CARE IN SASKATCHEWAN. THEY BUILT HOSPITALS AND STARTED A MEDICAL SCHOOL, PROVIDED FREE AIR AMBULANCE SERVICE AND FREE DENTAL AND MEDICAL CARE FOR PREGNANT WOMEN AND SENIORS. FINALLY, IN 1961, WHEN TOMMY WAS 57 YEARS OLD, THE MEDICAL CARE INSURANCE ACT WAS PASSED, GIVING FULL MEDICAL CARE FOR EVERY PERSON IN SASKATCHEWAN.

TOMMY WAS ASKED TO BE THE LEADER OF THE NATIONAL CCF, NOW NAMED THE NEW DEMOCRATIC PARTY (NDP). HE MADE HIS MARK IN THE HOUSE OF COMMONS IN OTTAWA AS A GREAT DEBATER AND A MAN OF STRONG PRINCIPLE, ALWAYS PUSHING THE GOVERNMENT IN POWER TO MAKE LIFE BETTER FOR ORDINARY CANADIANS. HE WAS WELL LIKED, KNOWN FOR HIS WIT AND HUMOUR.

TOMMY'S DREAM CAME TRUE ON JULY 1, 1968, WHEN PARLIAMENT VOTED TO BRING MEDICARE TO EVERY CANADIAN. PEOPLE CALLED HIM THE FATHER OF MEDICARE.

HE DIED OF CANCER IN 1986 AT THE AGE OF EIGHTY-ONE.

TOMMY DOUGLAS ALWAYS SAID, "YOU MEASURE YOUR LIFE NOT BY WHAT YOU GET, BUT BY WHAT YOU GIVE." HE GAVE EVERYTHING HE HAD TO SEE CANADA SITTING LIKE A LITTLE JEWEL AT THE TOP OF THE CONTINENT.

IN 2004, IN A NATIONAL CBC TELEVISION VOTE, TOMMY DOUGLAS WAS NAMED THE GREATEST CANADIAN OF ALL TIME BY PEOPLE ACROSS THE COUNTRY.

HIS FORMER CHURCH IN WEYBURN IS NOW THE T. C. DOUGLAS CALVARY CENTRE FOR PERFORMING ARTS.

BERYL YOUNG, STORY

BERYL YOUNG IS THE AUTHOR OF SEVEN BOOKS FOR CHILDREN. SHE WRITES NOVELS, BIOGRAPHIES, AND PICTURE BOOKS, INCLUDING *WISHING STAR SUMMER, CHARLIE: A HOME CHILD'S LIFE IN CANADA, WOULD SOMEONE PLEASE ANSWER THE PARROT!, FOLLOW THE ELEPHANT, MILES TO GO, A BOY FROM ACADIE: ROMÉO LEBLANC'S JOURNEY TO RIDEAU HALL* AND *SHOW US WHERE YOU LIVE, HUMPBACK*.

AMONG MANY AWARD NOMINATIONS, HER BOOKS HAVE WON THE RAINFOREST OF READING READER'S CHOICE AWARD (2014), THE B.C. CHOCOLATE LILY READER'S CHOICE AWARD (2012) AND THE U.S. SILVER MOONBEAM MEDAL (2010) (2019). BERYL'S LATEST BOOK *SHOW US WHERE YOU LIVE, HUMPBACK* RECEIVED A STARRED REVIEW FROM KIRKUS IN APRIL 2021.

BERYL LIVES IN VANCOUVER AND HAS THREE CHILDREN AND FOUR GRANDCHILDREN. SHE DEDICATES THIS BOOK TO ED BROADBENT WITH THANKS FOR HIS LIFELONG COMMITMENT TO SOCIAL DEMOCRACY.

Beryl & Walter were my neighbours in 1974-80's in Victoria

WWW.BERYLYOUNG.COM

JOAN STEACY, ILLUSTRATIONS

JOAN STEACY GREW UP IN SOUTHERN ONTARIO, AND IS A GRADUATE OF SHERIDAN COLLEGE, THE ONTARIO COLLEGE OF ART & DESIGN UNIVERSITY, AND THE UNIVERSITY OF VICTORIA. WITH HER HUSBAND KEN STEACY SHE CO-CREATED THE COMICS AND GRAPHIC NOVELS PROGRAM AT CAMOSUN COLLEGE IN VICTORIA, BC, WHERE SHE TAUGHT FROM 2012-2020.

JOAN IS ALSO THE AUTHOR/ILLUSTRATOR OF *SO, THAT'S THAT!* A BIOGRAPHY OF HER FATHER, A SCRAP-METAL DEALER WHO LIVED TO BE 100 YEARS OLD. SHE ALSO ILLUSTRATED A SHORT STORY FOR *A MINYEN YIDN*, A COLLECTION OF STORIES ABOUT LIFE IN THE SHTETL BY TRINA ROBBINS. HER FIRST GRAPHIC NOVEL *AURORA BOREALICE: A GRAPHIC MEMOIR*, WAS PUBLISHED BY CONUNDRUM PRESS IN 2019, AND WAS LISTED AS ONE OF "TEN CANADIAN COMICS TO READ RIGHT NOW" BY THE CBC.

WWW.JOANSTEACY.COM

A Boy Named Tommy Douglas
© Midtown Press, 2022

ISBN 978-1-988242-41-5 (print)
ISBN 978-1-988242-44-6 (PDF)
ISBN 978-1-988242-45-3 (EPUB)

Legal deposit: 1st quarter 2022
Printed in China by H&C Printing Center

Editor: Louis Anctil
Assistant: Daniel Anctil
Layout and production: Ken Steacy

Library and Archives Canada Cataloguing in Publication

Title: A Boy Named Tommy Douglas / Beryl Young ; illustrated by Joan Steacy.
Names: Young, Beryl, author. | Steacy, Joan, illustrator.
Description: Issued also in French under title: Jeunesse de Tommy Douglas.
Identifiers: Canadiana 20210292512 | ISBN 9781988242415 (hardcover)
Subjects: LCSH: Douglas, T. C. (Thomas Clement),
1904-1986—Childhood and youth—Juvenile literature.
| LCSH: Premiers (Canada)—Saskatchewan—Biography—Juvenile literature.
| LCGFT: Biographies.
Classification: LCC FC3525.1.D68 Y68 2021 | DDC j971.24/03092—dc23

Midtown Press thanks the Douglas-Coldwell Foundation
for supporting the publication of this book.

Midtown Press